James Payn

**Coridon's Song and other Verses**

From Various Sources

James Payn

**Coridon's Song and other Verses**
*From Various Sources*

ISBN/EAN: 9783337006044

Printed in Europe, USA, Canada, Australia, Japan

Cover: Foto ©Thomas Meinert / pixelio.de

More available books at **www.hansebooks.com**

# CORIDON'S SONG

*And other Verſes*

## FROM VARIOUS SOURCES

*With Illuſtrations by*

## HUGH THOMSON

*And an Introduction by*

## AUSTIN DOBSON

London

MACMILLAN AND CO.

AND NEW YORK

1894

A JOURNEY TO EXETER.

# INTRODUCTION

" *We, that are very old*"—*to borrow a phrase
from the immortal Isaac Bickerstaff—must re-
member how, over thirty years ago, followed to Robert
Browning's " Men and Women" the same author's
single volume of " Dramatis Personæ." It was a
brief collection, but it included the Master in all
his moods. For those who looked for " something
craggy to break their minds upon," there were
"James Lee's Wife" and " Dîs Aliter Visum" ;
for the mere lovers of poetry, there were " Rabbi
Ben Ezra," " Abt Vogler," the curious speculations
of Caliban upon Setebos, the magnificent narrative,
" supposed of Pamphylax, the Antiochene," entitled
" A Death in the Desert." Other pieces there were
again in that slender list of twenty, which have
since become household words in English Literature.
But among the lighter efforts was one in particular
which lingers in the mind of the present preface-
writer. It was the fancy called " A Likeness."
In the critical record its part is only a modest one.
Eight lines are all that Mrs. Sutherland Orr*

*devotes to it in her excellent manual, yet it has haunted one idle brain for a quarter of a century and more. And it is not so much its central idea which endures, as the skilful presentment of that idea, with its revel of rhyme—its " mark ace" and " cigar-case," its " alas ! mine" and "jasmine," its "keepsake" and " leaps, ache" (surely this last is as neat as Calverley's historical " dovetail" and " love tale".!)*—tours de force *which, to minds then less familiar with such dexterities, seemed scarcely short of miraculous. Perhaps, in the present day, it might be hinted that—for the modern rules of the game—the license of rhyming on proper names was used too freely. But this is to seek knots in a reed: and the lines at once regain their ancient charm to the votary who renews his study of them :—*

> " I keep my prints, an imbroglio,
>   Fifty in one portfolio.
>   When somebody tries my claret,
>   We turn round chairs to the fire,
>   Chirp over days in a garret,
>   Chuckle o'er increase of salary,
>   Taste the good fruits of our leisure.
>   Talk about pencil and lyre,
>   And the National Portrait Gallery :
>   Then I exhibit my treasure."

" *Talk of the National Portrait Gallery," only necessary in Browning's case for the fitter exhibition of his leading idea, would not, by the way, be ill-timed at the present moment, when, at last, there is some nearing prospect of the transfer, at*

*least to " an ampler ether," if not to "a diviner
air," of the art-treasures so long buried in a corner
at Bethnal Green.    But it is not of Mr. George
Scharf's portraits, or of their new Valhalla at
Trafalgar Square, that we now purpose to speak :
it is rather of the "pencil and lyre" in the poet's
preceding line.    The lyre here is the lyre of Gay,
of Swift, of Fielding—of that supreme " inheritor
of unfulfilled renown," the imperishable " Anon.":
the pencil is one already exercised successfully on
" Cranford," and " Our Village," and Goldsmith's
" Vicar"—the pencil of Mr.* HUGH THOMSON.    *If
the reader cannot " chuckle with us over increase of
salary," or (in retrospect) "chirp over days in a
garret," he can certainly pause for a space while we
"exhibit our treasure" ; and, as from a visionary
portfolio, draw forth the pictures and poems which
follow.    Only, seeing that the accomplished Artist may
read this " Introduction," we shall spare his blushes
by letting his pleasant sketches speak for themselves,
confining our office in the main to running comment
on the verses he has chosen for embellishment.*

Coridon's
Song,
pp. 1-17.

Integros    accedere    fontes,    atque
haurire—*seems    to    have    been    Mr.
Thomson's motto in his earliest selections,
for it is in Walton's " Angler" that he
finds his first sources of inspiration.    Of the
author of the song which Coridon the Country man
sings to Piscator and Master Peter, we know but
little, so little that it has even been profanely
suggested that his name should be Harris rather*

*than John Chalkhill, that reputed "Acquaintant of Edmund Spenser," and assumed composer of the "Pastoral History in smooth and easie Verse" which Walton put forth in 1683 under the title of "Thealma and Clearchus." Indeed, in some aids to learning, the book is roundly ascribed to Walton himself. But the modern investigator—who must always be meddling—has discovered there was actually existent in Walton's day a "Jo. Chalkhill, Gent.," who probably wrote verse, easy and otherwise ; and who, in spite of insinuations to the contrary, may really have been the inventor of this most desirable carol with its artless—*

> "heigh trolollie lollie loe,
> heigh trolollie lee,"

*and its new-old, old-new variation upon that time-honoured and delusive contrast between the Country and the Town which hath ever been the dream of those who "study to be quiet" :—*

> "For Courts are full of flattery,
> As hath too oft been tried ;
> heigh trolollie lollie loe,
> heigh trolollie lee,
> The City full of wantonness,
> and both are full of pride :
> Then care away,
> and wend along with me."

*" I shall love you for it as long as I know you," says honest Piscator. " I would you were a brother of the Angle, for a companion that is cheerful and free from swearing and scurrilous discourse, is*

*worth gold." " I love (he says once more) such mirth as does not make friends ashamed to look upon one another next morning" — a sentiment to which, were not the idea as old as Plato, one might fancy a resemblance in the later " mirth that, after, no repenting draws" of a certain austere John Milton. And so farewell, Master Coridon! Yours was a good song, and a merry, whoever be the author!*

It is from another self-proclaimed *"acquaintant" of the poet of the "Faerie Queene" that Piscator borrows his reply—a reply for which (according to the flattered Coridon) "Anglers are all beholding." Piscator's song, he himself tells us, was lately composed "at my request by Mr.* William Basse, *one that has made the choice Songs of the* Hunter in his carrere, *and of* Tom of Bedlam, *and many others of note." Time has dealt capriciously with this same William Basse. He was the friend of Browne and Wither and Ben Jonson, as well as of Spenser and Walton ; and when Shakespeare died, he wrote upon him an elegy wherein he bids him make his fourfold bed with Chaucer and Beaumont and Spenser—*

The Angler's Song, pp. 19-39.

> "Vntill Doomesdaye, for hardly will a fift
> Betwixt y⁸ day and yᵗ by Fate be slayne,
> For whom your Curtaines may be drawn againe"

*—a sentiment which, besides something of the spacious Elizabethan spirit, has also the merit of a not-discredited prediction. Yet the bulk of*

*Basse's work, unpublished during his life, re-*
*mained uncollected until last year, when he was born*
*out of due time in Mr. Warwick Bond's handsome*
*and scholarly edition. On the whole, however, it is*
*impossible to regard him as anything but a diluted*
*Spenserian. His flat pastoral fertility is more curious*
*than edifying, and prompts the suspicion that there*
*must have been just a touch of friendly log-rolling*
*about Walton's praise of his lyric gift, since it is not*
*greatly conspicuous in the pair of pieces mentioned,*
*neither of which excels the " Angler's Song." And*
*even in that the weightiest line is the first ("As*
*inward love breeds outward talk"). Still—leaving*
*open the question whether your thorough-paced*
*fisherman can really read at his craft—one must*
*confess a " contemplative" ease in the stanza—*

> " Of recreation there is none
> So free as fishing is alone ;
> All other pastimes do no less
> Than mind and body both possess ;
> My hand alone my work can do,
> So I can fish and study too."

" Who liveth
so merry,"
pp. 41-52.

*The " Compleat Angler" comes about*
*midway between the next two selections.*
*" Who liveth so merry" is from the*
*" Deuteromelia" of 1609, the date of*
*Shakespeare's " Sonnets": " Come, Sweet Lass,"*
*from " Pills to Purge Melancholy," which brings*
*us nigh to Dryden's " Fables" and 1700. The*
*" Deuteromelia" is a thin quarto of some fifteen*
*leaves, with a preface that might have been written*
*by Holofernes. Vt Mel Os, sic Cor melos afficit,*

*& reficit—says a motto in its highly elaborate title-page; and it was printed at London for Thomas Adams, dwelling in Paule's Church-yard "at the signe of the white Lion." The author was one Thomas Ravenscroft, sometime chorister of Paul's and graduate of Cambridge, whose "4-part psalms" were considered by that eminent connoisseur, Mr. Samuel Pepys, to be "most admirable musique." Already, earlier in 1609, Ravenscroft had published a series of rounds and canons entitled "Pammelia," of which "Deuteromelia" is the sequel. Turning its pages, one comes upon the lively catch of "Hold thy peace, thou knave," which Feste the Clown, and Sir Toby Belch, and Sir Andrew Aguecheek sing together in Act II. of "Twelfth Night"—a catch, as Sir Toby says, calculated to "draw three souls out of one weaver." A later ditty given in the book suggested the title borne by a famous chronicle of Mr. Rudyard Kipling :—*

"Wee be Souldiers three,
*Pardona moy ie vous an pree,*
Lately come forth of the low country
With neuer a penny of mony.
*Fa la la la lantido dilly.*"

*(The French of Flanders, it should be observed, apparently left something to be desired in the matter of spelling.) Then follows at p. 18, with its pleasant suggestion of old street cries and open-air callings, the "Freemen's Song" for four voices that Mr. Thomson has here illustrated, the moral of which seems to lie in the lines—*

" Who liveth so merry, and maketh such sport,
As those that be of the poorest sort?"

—*a point clearly open to argument.  It is not
true under Victoria : probably it was only poetically
true under " Eliza and our James."*

" Would you have a love-song, or a
"Come,
Sweet Lass,"   song of good life ?"—asks the Clown of
pp 53 63.    Sir Toby in that comedy of Shakespeare
to which we have already referred.
*And Olivia's reprobate uncle unhesitatingly declares
for a love-song, to which his led-captain, Sir Andrew,
with the exaggeration of the imitator, further adds
that he " cares not for good life."  Our next dip in
the lyric lucky-bag must assuredly have satisfied them
both.  It is " amatorious" enough for Sir Toby ;
and as an* Invitation à la Danse *should have had
special attractions for that expert in " Lavoltas high
and swift Corantos," his companion.  (Sir Andrew's
leg, we all know, did " indifferent well in a flame-
coloured stock.")  " Come, Sweet Lass " is apparently
one of the innumerable performances of that prolific
Tom D'Urfey, whose words, married to the music of
Purcell and Blow and Farmer, were once so well
known to our ancestors.  " He has been the delight
of the most polite companies and conversations, from
the beginning of king Charles the Second's reign to
our present times," says Addison in the " Guardian";
and Pope, in his Binfield boyhood, tells his friend
Cromwell that D'Urfey is "your only poet of toler-
able reputation in this country."  Over his volumin-
ous plays and farces, which Collier justly attacked,*

*Oblivion has discreetly "scattered her poppy"; but not a few of his songs still linger in our anthologies. One of the last testimonies to their popularity in his own day is contained in Gay's " Shepherd's Week." The references in the third and fourth lines are to D'Urfey's burlesque opera called " Wonders in the Sun," and his " ode" of the " Newmarket Horse Race" :—*

> "A while, O *D—y*, lend an Ear or twain,
> Nor, though in homely Guise, my Verse disdain,
> Whether thou seek'st new Kingdoms in the Sun,
> Whether thy Muse does at *New-Market* run,
> Or does with Gossips at a Feast regale,
> And heighten her Conceits with Sack and Ale,
> Or else at Wakes with *Joan* and *Hodge* rejoice,
> Where *D—y's* Lyricks swell in every Voice,
> Yet suffer me, thou Bard of wondrous Meed,
> Amid thy Bays to weave this rural Weed."

*According to the notes to Gay's Pastorals in the admirable edition of the late Mr. John Underhill, it appears that D'Urfey supplied the words to two other old songs mentioned by Gay, " Gillian of Croydon" and " Sawney Scot." Many who could sing, and many who could not, must have blessed that tuneful memory.*

Morning in London, pp. 65-79. *When Tom D'Urfey was buried in 1723 at St. James's, Piccadilly (where there is a tablet to his memory), Steele followed him to his grave. It was in Steele's then new periodical, the " Tatler," that first appeared the piece which here succeeds to " Come, Sweet Lass." Swift's " Morning in London " (or,*

*more strictly, " Morning in Town"), which Addison
is supposed to have sent to " Mr. Bickerstaff" from
Dublin with some of his own contributions to his
friend's venture, is leagues removed from the
previous verses. " An ingenious kinsman of mine"
—says Steele introducing it—" has run into a way
perfectly new, and described things exactly as they
happen: he never forms fields, or nymphs, or
groves, where they are not; but makes the incidents
just as they really appear." Swift, in short, is one
of the earliest of the realists, with much of their
merit and most of their defects. Nothing could be
surer-sighted than his inspection of the " slipshod
'prentice," the mop-whirling maid (whom he uses
again in the* City Shower), *the " youth with broomy
stumps" (observe the nice distinction between "broomy
stumps" and " stumpy broom"), the small-coal man,
the bailiffs, and all the sordid rest. But his photo-
graph of these things is taken from the seamy side,
and, like his latter-day disciples, he dwells upon this by
preference. Neither Steele nor Addison, one would
think, could have left this picture as it is. They
might perhaps have missed its microscopic view of
the mean and squalid; but they would undoubtedly
have added some touch of red-veined humanity to
warm the composition—a pretty girl seen smiling at
her glass—a child wondering in its bed at the
birth of a new day. We are apt to think that
Swift's contemporaries were blinder to his faults
than we are. But the Anglo-Gallic Annotator of
the " Babillard" was perfectly right when he con-
demned the petty range of the ideas. And it is not*

*necessary to contend with Johnson that, since "such a number of particulars could never have been assembled by the power of recollection," Swift must have noted down what he observed. On the contrary, Steele, in penning a little caveat against possible imitators of these particular verses, goes partway towards improvising the material himself. "I bar," he says, "all descriptions of the Evening; as, a medley of verses signifying grey peas are now cried warm . . . . or of Noon; as, that fine ladies and great beaux are just yawning out of their windows in Pall-Mall."*

*One of these imitators, in a better sense,*

A Journey to Exeter, pp. 81-115.

*was the poet of the pleasant rhyming epistle which follows Swift's Dutch picture. In the advertisement to "Trivia," Gay himself admits his indebtedness for "several hints" to Dr. Swift; and indeed it has always been supposed that "Morning in Town" and the "City Shower" supplied the initial suggestion for that poem. In the order of Gay's productions, the "Journey to Exeter" comes just before "Trivia." For reasons best known to the Artist, though doubtless sufficient, the introductory lines to Richard Boyle, Earl of Burlington, upon whose prompting, and at whose cost, the little trip was undertaken, are here omitted :—*

"While you, my Lord, bid stately piles ascend,
Or in your *Chiswick* bow'rs enjoy your friend ;
Where *Pope* unloads the boughs *within his reach*
The purple vine, blue plumb, and blushing peach ;
I journey far."

*b*

" *Within his reach*," *we have always supposed to be a sly stroke at the minute stature of the great Alexander. But Gay does not spare his own defects :—*

"You knew *fat* Bards might tire,
And, mounted, sent me forth your trusty Squire."

*Who the traveller's " two companions" were, history has not related, though he calls one Grævius:—*

" Now o'er true *Roman* way our horses sound,
*Grævius* would kneel, and kiss the sacred ground ;"

*and a line or two higher he speaks of sketching them both at Dorchester as they snored in their elbow chairs. There are many drawings by Pope extant ; what would one not give for this solitary* croquis *of Gay ! But in default of pictures with the pencil, the poem abounds in those pen sketches which are still the freshest legacy of the bard of " The Beggar's Opera." We seem to see the pigeon-feeding Solomon of Turnham Green, as he has been revealed to the Artist and denied to the antiquary ; we watch the travellers riding warily over Bagshot Heath—*

" Where broken gamesters oft' repair their loss ; "

*we taste the red trout and " rich metheglin " of Steele's borough of Stockbridge, the lobster and " unadulterate wine " of Morecombe ; we spell out on the road from Honiton—*

" Where finest lace industrious lasses weave,"

*the rhyming sign of that " Hand and Pen " where the rain-drenched party take shelter. And at Axminster*

*there is the "pretty washermaiden" (as Mr. Henley
would call her) of whom Mr. Thomson has contrived
so charming a portrait.   But why, O why! has he
forborne to draw for us that most impressive local
celebrity, the female barber?*

> " The weighty golden chain adorns her neck,
> And three gold rings her skilful hand bedeck :
> Smooth o'er our chin her easy fingers move,
> Soft as when *Venus* strok'd the beard of *Jove*."

*Twelve years had passed away when
John Gay composed the brief and better-
known song which follows.   Since, in
1728, William Hogarth painted, for
William Blake eventually to engrave, the likeness of
Captain Macheath "between his two Deborahs"—
the Polly and Lucy of the "Beggar's Opera"—the
couplet "How happy could I be with either, Were
t'other dear Charmer away," has been an almost
indispensable formula for the expression of mascu-
line indecision in presence of conflicting feminine
attractions.   Nor has it been employed in this way
alone, for it has done service in many another
fashion of dilemma.   To take but the latest example,
only the other day it was triumphantly pressed by
Sir William Harcourt into a discussion on the
business of the House of Commons, when—to the
amusement of that august body—Mr. Goschen neatly
countered its Leader by completing the quotation :—*

"How happy
could I be,"
pp. 117-123.

> " But while you thus tease me together,
> To neither a word will I  say."

*b* 2

*For this reason, it may be, Mr. Thomson has treated the song, less as an extract from the famous piece which made " Gay rich, and Rich gay," than as a cosmopolitan utterance—a cry wrung from the heart of embarrassed male humanity. It is, in fact, one of those " Eternal Verities " of which Carlyle was wont to speak—as old as Adam, as young as yesterday.*

"A Hunting we will go," pp. 125-139.

*Over Fielding's "Hunting Song" and " Oh! dear! what can the matter be?" we may pass more rapidly. If the play of " Don Quixote in England," from Act II. of which the first is taken, really included these verses when it was sketched by its author at Leyden, it follows that his gifts as a song-writer must have been manifested more early and more enduringly than his dramatic powers. Fielding's comedies have never held their ground; but this rollicking ditty of men and dogs, set to the fine old air " There was a jovial beggar," is still good to sing and to hear. The same play contains a suggestion of another famous lyric:—*

> "Oh the roast beef of old England,
>     And old England's roast beef!"

*And one of the verses in " The dusky night rides down the sky" supplies a useful note to the " Spectator." Says the song: -*

> "A brushing fox in yonder wood,
>     Secure to find we seek ;
> For why, I carry'd, sound and good,
>     A cartload there last week."

*This is precisely the practice of which Budgell accuses the provident Sir Roger de Coverley: "Indeed the Knight does not scruple to own among his most intimate Friends, that in order to establish his Reputation this Way [as a Fox-killer], he has secretly sent for great Numbers of them [Foxes] out of other Counties, which he used to turn loose about the Country by Night, that he might the better signalise himself in their Destruction the next Day."*

"Oh! dear! what can the matter be?" pp. 141-149.

*Upon "Oh! dear! what can the matter be?"—both words and tune of which are anonymous—little comment can be needed beyond that afforded by the illustrations. It is still among the most familiar of its old-fashioned kind, and may continue to supply subjects to the* genre *painter for another century or two.*

Sir Dilberry Diddle, pp. 151-163.

*"Captain (of Militia) Sir Dilberry Diddle"—the last upon our list—belongs, we should imagine, to the epoch of the "Seven Years' War." Sir Dilberry is clearly the growth of that chronic dread of invasion which prompted not only Hogarth's "France" and "England," but many another valiant pictorial gibe at the frog-eating "Mounseers" who were always threatening to cross over with their friars, and their Popish racks and thumbscrews, to build their black monasteries within sound of Bow Bells. Like John Gilpin, he is to be ranked with those train-band captains "of credit and renown" who furnished such frank laughter to the Footes and Colmans*

*of their day. His actual exploits, as those satirists hinted, rarely went, in all probability, much beyond the investment of a hay-stack or the occupation of an alehouse, for the "flat-bottomed boats" so frequently mentioned by Goldsmith and others never found their way into English ports, nor have we to this day—in the mixed metaphor of the "Gazetteer"—"lain down to be saddled with wooden shoes." But however we estimate the precise value of what Mr. Hosea Biglow styles "milishy gloary," there is no need why we should mock at an honourable patriotic instinct, even in a citizen-soldier. If the French had come, doubtless Sir Dilberry would have fought as well waking as he did asleep. In any case, let us not begrudge him his long nap under the short apron of his excellent lady—surely one of the most original of Mr. Thomson's creations!*

*Part of the foregoing Introduction—an Introduction of necessity somewhat invertebrate and discursive—was written in the West of Scotland. On the grey and ancient island of Iona, the author, with the rest of his party, followed the appointed Guide in the round of its venerable ruins. The Tale was of Macbeth and King Fergus; of the Cross of St. Martin of Tours (who divided his cloak with the beggar); of the stone pillow of St. Columba (in its cage of iron); of the rudely carved griffin which served as model for the monster at Temple Bar. Meanwhile, in pauses of that instructive oration—perhaps even during its progress—the eyes of the listeners wandered vaguely to the clear blue over-*

*head; to the patches of particoloured lichen; to
the tufts of salt-fed spleenwort "in the crannied
wall"; to the fringe of freckled, bare-legged children
with sea-urchins and necklets of shells for sale;
to the endless and inexhaustible detail, often more
articulate than history, more persuasive than fact.
The function of the preface-making Dryasdust is
not unlike that of the topographical cicerone. He
may recapitulate dates, and recount anecdotes; but
his restless audience will seek for themselves, and
will probably select what they admire where they have
not been invited to search for it. With the conviction
that such cannot lack for individual choice in the
abundant invention of the designs which follow,
the writer of these preliminary pages cheerfully
absolves them if they should now turn—even with
a sense of relief — from the comment to the text
and illustrations.*

*AUSTIN DOBSON.*

EALING, *September* 1894.

# CONTENTS

# LIST OF ILLUSTRATIONS

## *Coridon's Song*

## *The Angler's Song*

## A Journey to Exeter

## "*How happy could I be with either*"

## "*A Hunting we will go*"

## "*Oh! dear! what can the matter be?*"

## Sir Dilberry Diddle

# Coridon's Song

from *Walton's Complete Angler*

# Coridon's Song

h, the sweet contentment
The countryman doth find!
Heigh trolollie lollie loe,
Heigh trolollie lollie lee.
That quiet contemplation
Possesseth all my mind;
Then care away,
And wend along with me.

# Coridon's Song

*For Courts are full of flattery*
*As hath too oft been tried ;*
        *Heigh trolollie lollie loe,*
        *Heigh trolollie lollie lee.*
*The city full of wantonnefs,*
*And both are full of pride :*
        *Then care away,*
        *And wend along with me.*

# Coridon's Song

But oh! the honeſt countryman
Speaks truly from his heart;
    Heigh trolollie lollie loe,
    Heigh trolollie lollie lee.
His pride is in his tillage,
His horſes and his cart;
    Then care away,
    And wend along with me.

# Coridon's Song

Our clothing is good sheep-skins,
Grey ruffet for our wives;
    Heigh trolollie lollie loe,
    Heigh trolollie lollie lee.
'Tis warmth, and not gay clothing,
That doth prolong our lives;
    Then care away,
    And wend along with me.

The ploughman, though he labour hard,
Yet on the holiday,
    Heigh trolollie lollie loe,
    Heigh trolollie lollie lee.
No emperor so merrily
Doth pass his time away ;
    Then care away,
    And wend along with me.

# Coridon's Song

To recompen*f*e our tillage,
The heavens afford us showers;
    Heigh trolollie lollie loe,
    Heigh trolollie lollie lee.
And for our sweet refre*f*hments
The earth affords us bowers;
    Then care away,
    And wend along with me.

# Coridon's Song

# Coridon's Song

The cuckoo and the nightingale
Full merrily do sing,
    Heigh trolollie lollie loe,
    Heigh trolollie lollie lee.
And with their pleasant roundelays
Bid welcome to the spring ;
    Then care away,
    And wend along with me.

*This is not half the happiness*
*The countryman enjoys ;*
    *Heigh trololie lollie loe,*
    *Heigh trolollie lollie lee.*
*Though others think they have as much,*
*Yet he that says so lies ;*
    *Then come away, turn*
    *Countryman with me.*

# The Angler's Song

# The Angler's Song

A s inward love breeds outward talk,
The hound some praise, and some
the hawk ;

## The Angler's Song

*Some, better pleafed with private sport,*
*Ufe tennis; some a mistrefs court;*
*But thefe delights I neither wifh*
*Nor envy, while I freely fifh.*

# The Angler's Song

# The Angler's Song

Who hunts, doth oft in danger ride;
Who hawks, lures oft both far and wide;
Who uses games shall often prove

# The Angler's Song

*A loſer ; but who falls in love*
*Is fetter'd in fond Cupid's snare :*
*My angle breeds me no such care.*

# The Angler's Song

## The Angler's Song

*Of recreation there is none*
*So free as fishing is alone;*
*All other pastimes do no less*
*Than mind and body both possess;*
*My hand alone my work can do,*
*So I can fish and study too.*

I care not, I, to fish in seas—
Fresh rivers most my mind do please,
Whose sweet calm course I contemplate,
And seek in life to imitate:
In civil bounds I fain would keep,
And for my past offences weep.

# The Angler's Song

And when the timorous trout I wait
To take, and he devours my bait,
How poor a thing, sometimes I find,
Will captivate a greedy mind;
And when none bite, I praise the wise,
Whom vain allurements ne'er surprise.

D

The Angler's Song

But yet, though while I fish I fast,
I make good fortune my repast;
And thereunto my friend invite,
In whom I more than that delight;
Who is more welcome to my dish
Than to my angle was my fish.

*As well content no prize to take,*
*As ufe of taken prize to make:*
*For so our Lord was pleafed, when*
*He fifhers made fifhers of men:*
*Where (which is in no other game)*
*A man may fifh and praife His name.*

*The firſt men that our Saviour dear*
*Did chooſe to wait upon Him here,*
*Bleſſ'd fiſhers were, and fiſh the laſt*
*Food was that He on earth did taſte ;*
*I therefore ſtrive to follow thoſe*
*Whom He to follow Him hath choſe.*

# "Who liveth so merry"

*"Who liveth so merry"*

Who liveth so merry in all this land
    As doth the poor widow that selleth the
        sand ?
And ever she singeth as I can guefs,
" Will you buy a—ny sand, a—ny sand,
    mif—trefs ? "

42

*The broom-man maketh his living most sweet,*
*With carrying of brooms from street to street;*
*Who would desire a pleasanter thing*
*Than all day long doing nothing but sing?*

*Who liveth so merry*

*The chimney-sweeper all the long day,*
*He singeth and sweepeth the soot away:*
*Yet when he comes home, although he be weary,*
*With his sweet wife he maketh himself full*
  *merry.*

47

*Who liveth so merry*

*The cobbler he sits cobbling till noon,*
*And cobbleth his shoes till they be done,*
*Yet doth he not fear, and so doth say,*
*For he knows his work will soon decay.*

49

*Who liveth so merry*

*The merchant-man doth sail on the seas,*
*And lie on the shipboard with little eafe;*
*Always in doubt the rock is near,*
*How can he be merry and make good cheer?*

*The hufbandman all day goeth to plough,*
*And when he comes home he serveth his sow;*
*He moileth, and moileth all the long year,*
*How can he be merry and make good cheer?*

*The serving-man waiteth from street to street,*
*With blowing his nails and beating his feet;*
*And serveth for forty shillings a year,*
*How can he be merry and make good cheer?*

51

# Who liveth so merry

Who liveth so merry and maketh such sport,
As those that be of the poorest sort?
The poorest sort, wheresoever they be,
They gather together, by one, two, and three.

And every man will spend his penny,
What makes such a show among a great many?

(Bis.)
from Deuteromelia, 1609

# “Come Sweet Lass”

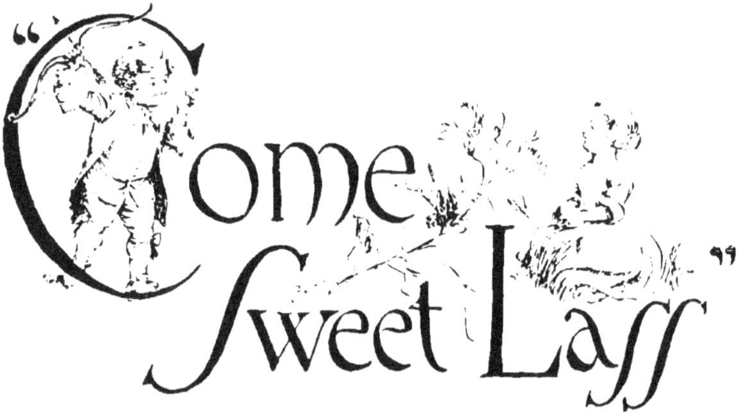

## "Come, sweet Lass"

Come, sweet lass ;
This bonny weather
Let's to-gether ;

*Come, sweet laſs*




*Come, sweet laſs*
*Let's trip upon the graſs,*

*Ev'ry where*
*Poor Jocky seeks his dear,*
*And unless you ap-pear,*
*He sees no beauty here.*

*On our green*
*The loons are sporting,*
*Piping, courting:*
*On our green*
*The blithest lads are seen:*
*There, all day,*
*Our lasses dance and play,*

*And ev'ry one is gay*
*But I, when you're away.*

a
Description
of

# Morning in LONDON.

# Morning in London

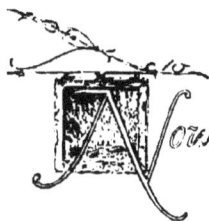

Now hardly here and there a hackney coach
Appearing show'd the ruddy morn's
approach.
The slipſhod 'prentice from his maſter's door
Had pared the dirt, and sprinkled round the
floor.

66

*Now Moll had whirl'd her mop with dexterous
airs,*
*Prepar'd to scrub the entry and the stairs,*

.

The youth with broomy stumps began to trace
The kennel's edge, where wheels had worn the
    place,

Morning in London

*Morning in London*

The small coal man was heard with cadence deep,
'Till drown'd in shriller notes of chimney-sweep ;

*Morning in London*

Duns at his Lordſhip's gate began to meet;
And brick-duſt Moll had scream'd through half the
    street.

Morning in London

## Morning in London

The turnkey now his flock returning sees
Duly let out a-nights to steal for fees ;
The watchful bailiffs take their silent stands,

*And schoolboys lag with satchels in their hands.*

A JOURNEY TO EXETER

81

'Twas on the day that city dames repair
  To take their weekly dose of Hyde-Park air;
  When forth we trot: no carts the roads infest
  For still on Sundays country horses rest.

.

82

83

*Thy gardens, Kensington, we leave unseen;*
*Through Hammersmith jog on to Turnham Green:*

84

*That Turnham-Green, which dainty pigeons fed,*
*But feeds no more: for Solomon is dead.*

Three dusty miles reach Brentford's tedious town,
For dirty streets and white-legg'd chickens known :
Thence o'er wide shrubby heaths, and furrow'd
    lanes,
We come, where Thames divides the meads of
    Staines.
We ferry'd o'er; for late the Winter's flood
Shook her frail bridge, and tore her piles of
    wood.
Prepar'd for war, now Bagshot Heath we crofs,
Where broken gamefters oft repair their lofs.

At Hartley Row the foaming bit we preſt,
While the fat landlord welcom'd ev'ry guest.
Supper was ended, healths the glaſſes crown'd,
Our hoſt extoll'd his wine at ev'ry round,
Relates the Juſtices' late meeting there
How many bottles drank, and what their cheer;
What lords had been his gueſts in days of
    yore,
And praiſed their wiſdom much, their drinking
    more.

91

Let travellers the morning vigils keep:
The morning rofe, but we lay faft afleep.
Twelve tedious miles we bore the sultry sun,
And Popham Lane was scarce in sight by one;
The straggling village harbour'd thieves of old,
'Twas here the stage-coach'd lafs refign'd her
    gold;
That gold which had in London purchaf'd
    gowns,
And sent her home a Belle to country towns.

93

Sutton we pafs, and leave her spacious down,
And with the setting sun reach Stockbridge town.
O'er our parch'd tongue the rich metheglin glides,
And the red dainty trout our knife divides.
Sad melancholy ev'ry vifage wears ;
What, no election come in seven long years !
Of all our race of Mayors, shall Snow alone
Be by Sir Richard's dedication known?
Our streets no more with tides of ale shall float,
Nor cobblers feaft three years upon one vote.
Next morn, twelve miles led o'er th'unbounded
   plain,
Where the cloak'd shepherd guides his fleecy
   train.
No leafy bow'rs a noon-day shelter lend,
Nor from the chilly dews at night defend :
With wondrous art, he counts the straggling flock,
And by the sun informs you what's a clock.

95

*How are our shepherds fall'n from ancient days!*
*No Amaryllis chants alternate lays;*
*From her no list'ning echoes learn to sing,*
*Nor with his reed the jocund valleys ring.*
*Here sheep the pasture hide, there harvests bend,*
*See Sarum's steeple o'er yon hill ascend;*
*Our horses faintly trot beneath the heat,*
*And our keen stomachs know the hour to eat.*

*Who can forsake thy walls, and not admire*
*The proud cathedral, and the lofty spire?*
*What sempstress has not proved thy scissors good?*
*From hence first came th' intriguing riding-hood.*
*Amid three boarding-schools well stock'd with*
  *misses*
*Shall three knight-errants starve for want of*
  *kisses?*
*O'er the green turf the miles slide swift away,*
*And Blandford ends the labours of the day.*

The morning rofe ; the supper reck'ning paid,
And our due fees difcharged to man and maid ;
The ready oftler near the stirrup stands,
And as we mount, our half-pence load his hands.

Now the steep hill fair Dorchefter o'erlooks,
Border'd by meads, and wafh'd by silver brooks.
Here sleep my two companions' eyes suppreft,
And propt in elbow-chairs they snoring reft :
I weary sit, and with my pencil trace
Their painful poftures, and their eyelefs face ;
Then dedicate each glafs to some fair name,
And on the safh the diamond scrawls my flame.

103

Now o'er true Roman way our horses sound,
Gr*vius* would kneel, and kifs the
sacred ground.
On either side low fertile valleys lie,
The diftant profpects tire the travelling eye.
Through Bridport's stony lanes our rout we take,
And the proud steep defcend to Morcombe's lake.
As hearfes pafs'd, our landlord robbed the pall,
And with the mournful 'scutcheon hung his hall.
On unadulterate wine we here regale,
And strip the lobfter of his scarlet mail.

105

*We climb'd the hills, when starry night arose,*
*And Axminster affords a kind repose.*
*The maid subdu'd by fees, her trunk unlocks,*
*And gives the cleanly aid of dowlas smocks.*

107

Meantime our shirts her busy fingers rub,
While the soap lathers o'er the foaming tub.
We rise, our beards demand the barber's art;
A female enters, and performs the part.
The weighty golden chain adorns her neck,
And three gold rings her skilful hand bedeck;
Smooth o'er our chin her easy fingers move,
Soft as when Venus strok'd the beard of Jove.
Now from the steep, 'midst scatter'd cots and
    groves,
Our eye through Honiton's fair valley roves.

# A Journey to Exeter

Behind us soon the busy town we leave,
Where finest lace industrious lasses weave,
Now swelling clouds roll'd on; the rainy load
Stream'd down our hats, and smok'd along the
    road ;
When (O blest sight!) a friendly sign we spy'd,
Our spurs are slacken'd from the horse's side ;

III

For sure a civil hoſt the houſe commands,
Upon whoſe sign this courteous motto stands, —
" This is the ancient hand, and eke the pen ;
Here is for horſes hay, and meat for men."
How rhyme would flouriſh, did each son of fame
Know his own genius, and direct his flame !
Then he that could not Epic fights rehearſe,
Might sweetly mourn in Elegiac verſe.
But were his Muſe for Elegy unfit,
Perhaps a Diſtich might not strain his wit ;

If Epigram offend, his harmless lines
Might in gold letters swing on ale-house signs.
Then Hobbinol might propagate his bays
And Tuttle-fields record his simple lays ;
Where rhymes like these might lure the nurses'
    eyes
While gaping infants squall for farthing pies—
" Treat here, ye shepherds blithe, your damsels
    sweet,
For pies and cheesecakes are for damsels meet."

Then Maurus in his proper sphere might shine,
And these proud numbers grace great William's
    sign ; —
" This is the man, this the Nassovian, whom
I named the brave deliverer to come."
But now the driving gales suspend the rain,
We mount our steeds, and Devon's city gain.
Hail, happy native land !—but I forbear
What other counties must with envy hear.

115

"How happy could I be with either"

## "How happy could I be with either"

How happy could I be with either,
   Were t'other dear charmer a-way;

118

*But while you thus teaſe me to-gether*

120

*How happy could I be with either*




*To neither a word will I say.*

# A HUNTING
## WE WILL GO

## "A Hunting we will go"

The dusky night rides down the sky,
And ushers in the morn;
The Hounds all join in glorious cry,
The Hounds all join in glorious cry,

126

The huntsman winds his horn.
The huntsman winds his horn.
And  a hunting we will go,
A hunting we will go,
A hunting we will go,
A hunting we will go.

The wife around her husband throws
Her arms, and begs his stay ;
My dear, it rains, it hails, it snows,
You will not hunt to-day ?
But a hunting we will go,
A hunting we will go,
A hunting we will go,
A hunting we will go.

131

*A hunting we will go*




*A bruſhing fox in yonder wood,*
*Secure to find we seek ;*
*For why, I carried, sound and good,*
*A cartload there laſt week.*
*And a hunting we will go,*
*A hunting we will go,*
*A hunting we will go,*
*A hunting we will go.*

Away he goes, he flies the rout,
Their steeds all **spur** and switch;
Some are thrown **in,** and some thrown out,
And some thrown **in** the ditch.

A hunting we will go

But a hunting we will go,
A hunting we will go,
A hunting we will go,
A hunting we will go.

136

*A hunting we will go*

At length his strength to faintnefs worn,
Poor Reynard ceafes flight;
Then hungry, homeward we return,
To feaft away the night.
Then a drinking we will go,
A drinking we will go,
A drinking we will go,
A drinking we will go.

139

"Oh! Dear! What can the matter be?"

*h! dear! what can the matter be?*
*Dear! dear! what can the matter be?*
*Oh! dear! what can the matter be?*
*Johnny's so long at the fair.*

•

142

143

*Oh ! dear ! what can the matter be ?*

*He promiſ'd he'd buy me a fairing should pleaſe*
    *me,*
*And then for a kiſs, Oh ! he vow'd he would*
    *teaze me ;*
*He promiſ'd he'd bring me a bunch of blue*
    *ribbons*
*To tie up my bonny brown hair.*

L

Oh ! dear ! what can the matter be ?
Dear ! dear ! what can the matter be ?
Oh ! dear ! what can the matter be ?
Johnny's so long at the fair.

*He promis'd he'd bring me a basket of posies,*
*A garland of lilies, a garland of roses,*
*A little straw hat, to set off the blue ribbons*
*That tie up my bonny brown hair.*

Oh! dear! what can the matter be?

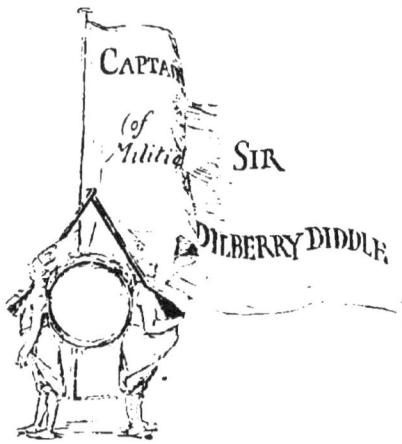

CAPTAIN

(of
Militia)

SIR

DILBERRY DIDDLE

# Sir Dilberry Diddle

f all the brave captains that ever were seen,
Appointed to fight by a king or a queen,
By a king or a queen appointed to fight,
Sure never a captain was like this brave
knight.

He pulled off his slippers and wrapper of
silk,
And, foaming as furious as whiskèd new
milk,
Says he to his lady, " My lady, I'll go :
My company calls me ; you must not say no."

# Sir Dilberry Diddle

*With eyes all in tears says my lady, says she,*
*"O cruel Sir Dilberry, do not kill* me !
*For I never will leave thee, but cling round thy*
*middle,*
*And die in the arms of Sir Dilberry Diddle."*

*Said Diddle again to his lady, " My dear,"*
*(And a white pocket-handkerchief wiped off a tear)*
*" To fight for thy charms in the hottest of wars*
*Will be joy ! Thou art Venus." Says she, " Thou*
*art Mars."*

## Sir Dilberry Diddle

By a place I can't mention, not knowing its name,
At the head of his company Dilberry came,
And the drums to the window call every eye
To see the defence of the nation pafs by.

Old Bible-faced women, through spectacles dim,
With hemming and coughing, cried " Lord, it is
    him ! "
While boys and the girls, who more clearly could
    see,
Cried, " Yonder's Sir Dilberry Diddle — that's
    he ! "

# Sir Dilberry Diddle

## Sir Dilberry Diddle

Of all the fair ladies that came to the show,
Sir Diddle's fair lady stood firſt in the row;
"Oh, how charming," says she, "he looks all in
    red:
How he turns out his toes, how he holds up his
    head!

"Do but see his cockade, and behold his dear gun,
Which shines like a looking-glaſs held in the sun!
Hear his word of command! 'tis so sweet, I am
    sure,
Each time I am tempted to call out—encore!"

159

The battle was over without any blows,
The heroes unharnefs and strip off their clothes;
The dame gives her captain a sip of rofe-water,
Then he, handing her into her coach, steps in
    after.

John's orders are special to drive very slow,
For fevers oft follow fatigues, we all know,
And prudently cautious, in Venus's lap,
Beneath her short apron, Mars takes a long nap.

# Sir Dilberry Diddle

*He dreamt, Fame reports, that he cut all the throats*
*Of the French as they landed in flat-bottomed*
*boats,*
*In his sleep if such dreadful deſtruction he makes,*
*What havock, ye gods! we shall have when he*
*wakes!*

www.ingramcontent.com/pod-product-compliance
Lightning Source LLC
Chambersburg PA
CBHW030840270326
41928CB00007B/1136